Days Gone By

Poetry and Writings by Michael B. Van Winkle

Some material has appeared in previous books by the author:
Cloudy Blue Adagio © 2002; *As Is A Flower* © 2005; *The Telling* © 2011.

Print ISBN: 978-1-66782-807-7
eBook ISBN: 978-1-66782-808-4

Printed in the United States of America on SFI Certified paper.

First Edition

Acknowledgement

With thanks to the Fates for their patience.

Contents

Love   ix

Beauty   29

Loss   45

Gratitude   61

Forgiveness   71

Discovery   77

Nights   111

Seasons   121

Child   131

Writings   141

LOVE

Warmth In Wetness

The silent, drifting snow
glided down from the heavens
in big wet flakes.
Arm in arm,
we escaped into the night,
pelted by soft crystal kisses
and whispering promises
that all lovers make.
Forever, I said.
Always, you pledged.
Hand in hand,
we walked on down the road,
our footsteps furrowing
the white immaculate,
certain the snow
would forever hide
our forbidden togetherness.

The Dance Of Souls

You are here! I see you, I feel you.
Heaven awaits the dance of souls.

We embrace, meld to golden light,
and whirl to God's sublime song.

Listen...close your eyes...
rejoice in the chorus,
rapture the violins,
kiss to soft harmonies.

We are one.

Two Clouds Kissing

Two clouds played above me
on a blue satin sheet.
Like shy young lovers
afraid to touch,
fearful of lust's fire,
they rolled and laughed
and stared and quickened.
In a sudden rush
of mutual abandon
they kissed.

Frog Song

Remember the night
when the moon was bright,
a saffron sliver
smiling on some distant river?

We listened in a trance
as frogs began their dance
to a timeless spring tune
that will end far too soon.

You waved your magic wand
over the little pond
to protect our secret place
and wish it eternal grace.

It was a great pleasure
to share this rare treasure
and complete our bliss
with a gentle, sweet kiss.

I Remember You

The fog is nature's lover…
billowing up from the bay below,
caressing the sea breezes,
swirling in dance sublime
to a waltz of mist and wind.

Black birch leaves sparkle
at the passing of fairy dew.
Goldenrod gleams in repose.
White phlox flowers bow low.
Crickets trumpet their approval.

Oh, mother, I see this beauty
through your eyes and senses.
You would have loved it here.
As I walk the field paths,
I feel you, I remember you.

Things She Gave Me

Could I have been so near to knowing,
so fearless in the quest,
had I not been born of you?
I think not.
For it was you who let me see
the pieces of my way.

Creatures great and small came first,
like dogs and fish and rabbits
and pigeons and horses and mice.

Flowers fragrant and bright were next,
like tulips and daisies and lilacs
and roses and daffodils and irises.

Colors from grandfather's palette blazed,
like cadmium and umber and ivory
and azure and russet and saffron.

Words from poets later stirred my soul,
like Brooke and Shelley and Keats
and Frost and Burns and Millay.

You gave me
creatures,
flowers,
colors,
and words.

You gave me life.

The Path

I wonder…
Old path worn smooth
by me, my dog, and time,
what trace of our being
will remain when
we are gone away?

It answers…

Memories? Awhile.
Pictures? Some.
Words? Few.

None of these are timeless.
But the love between
a man and his dog
will last forever.

Whiskers

Last night I felt your heart
beating hard against my own.
Up you climbed upon my lap
and promptly fell asleep,
your head resting on my shoulder.
The moment lasted a breath in time
but I will treasure the memory always.

My beautiful dog named Bugle,
thank you for trusting me so.
I would die a happy man
if the last thing I felt on Earth
was your whiskers tickling my cheek.

Now We Are Three

Little white dog, now we are three,
just Bugle and me and Mrs. B.
How happy you made us
when you came to our door,
green goo on your fluffy white snout!
You gave us comfort and love
and memories for a lifetime.
Face plants in the mud.
Ears flapping wildly in the wind
as you chased brother Busky
down the long forest trail.
Excited barking when signs pointed
to a walk at the close of day.
Quiet times on Dorothy's lap.
Licks galore from head to toe.
Pinecones carried round the block.
Last pee-pees in the cold of night,
and games you loved like ice cubes,
who-wants-a-bone, and carrot-carrot.
Brave you were, and fierce and proud.
You stood your ground.
You met death more than once
but found the will to live.

We miss you Cherie.
Find us again for it's here you belong
and here you will always find love.
Rest now in quiet. We await your return.

Ode To Old Dogs

Sweet Becky, I remember you well
curled up by the fire in the cold,
a lady pointer so gentle and kind,
you were always hard to scold.

Bear, your son, was next to stay,
and we loved his color black.
Happy he was to greet the bus
and guide us safely back.

Wildy then came and what a sight
were his wild dog colors to see!
Many a squirrel must have wondered
why he tore the bark from the tree.

It's memories that make a place so dear,
of love and life and laughter
and places walked, and lovers kissed,
and old dogs chasing after.

My Wary Sense Surrendered

I was very brave that night
to risk a climb up your favorite chair.
I planned each little step…
first a front paw to the cushion,
another to your side,
next a single back paw,
and last…a leap to a flop.
You caught me in your arms
and my wary sense surrendered
to the beating of your heart,
the touch of your loving hand,
the softness of your words
as you whispered my name
and rubbed my ears
the special way you always do.
I laid my head on your shoulder
and closed my eyes in peace.
You must know, true friend,
I have never felt more safe and loved.
When I am gone, as I must be,
remember this moment, remember the love.

You say I owe you nothing.
I say I owe you everything.
You gave me a name, a collar, a home with grass
and years to roam, chase, watch, and guard.

I will treasure the love I saw in your eyes
and the scent of your hand as I left you.
Now I await you at the bridge, ever looking,
ever joyful, ever sure that I will see your eyes again.

He Came To Me

First, it was the sound,
a soft rustle in the grass
at one of his favorite spots.
I turned to see the source
but there was nothing there.
Then, I smelled a scent
like none I had ever known.
Sweet pine, light, pure, perfect.
It lasted seconds, went, returned.

I opened my arms to greet him.
I closed my eyes and rubbed his ears,
itched his neck and scratched his back.
I took his head in my hands
and kissed him gently on his cheek.

In the pale night light, he came to me
my beautiful dog named Bugle.
Love brought you back
to say a final farewell.

Dew Tracks

Her jingling collar stirs me
on a humid Maine morn.
Six tags, some old, some new
rattle as the puppy shakes herself awake,
stretching, yawning and groaning
like a old dog stiff with years.

A stumbling pair of predawn explorers,
we wander down the deck stairs
into a sky still pink with rust and red
sketched on a hint of pale blue starlight.
Grass heavy with dew darkens my shoes,
seeps to my toes, and glistens on her paws
as we quietly walk the mown field paths.

It is an ancient ritual revisited,
this man and dog bond...
friend with friend,
love with love,
trust with trust,
making dew tracks together
and wondering what the day will bring.

Freedom In Her Eyes

Her brown eyes are on alert,
searching for a hint of what
our movements mean,
our words convey,
our smiles promise.

The jingle of keys,
hats on our heads,
shoes laced up,
coats buttoned tightly…
these are the telltale signs
of a ride in the car!

But there's mischief afoot
as she leaps from the seat
and waits on the leash
for a walk in the sun.

Today, we let this child free
to run the field, feel the wind,
hunt the critters, sniff the deer.

In a precious moment of realization,
she whipples her thanks,
prancing and leaping and circling
in pure dog joy.

We see the freedom in her eyes.

Dog In A Field

Head lifted high, wet nose to the wind,
cur tail curving and quivering,
she patrols the field with senses alert
to the chirp of a cricket,
the squeak of a chippy,
the flutter of a bird.

A distant woof from across the bay
distracts her briefly from the hunt.
Curious, she turns to the bark
and greets the canine connection
with lifted ears and a steady gaze
through soft brown eyes.

Lady Is Dreaming

Lady is dreaming of a daring dash
headlong into a thorny thicket
in futile pursuit of a rascal rodent
who chatters from his hidden hole.

The Ballad Of Whimpering Feebles

It happens every day to me
even though I pretend to flee.
I'm the Head Feeble like it or not
and I know that means diddlysquat
except to the Feebles who after chow
insist they need their beauty rest *now*.

So whimper and whine is their play
as they try to cajole me to upstairs sway,
but though I resist as long as I might,
I know in the end it's a true delight
to snuggle atop the covers with cuties
and enjoy the love of our two beauties.

Higher To The Sky

There! The light between the trees!
Hurry now, for beyond is a prize
of sight and soul and the peace
that comes from dreams.

Look! Someday we'll share a place
like this but higher to the sky.
A place to begin.
A place to end.

On a fine fall day when the woods
are aflame with sun and splendor,
walk to the crook in the high meadow
where the old wall turns to the west.
Bring a small stone from our garden
and fit it in the wall where you will.
Watch the sun surrender to dusk
over the view we loved so dear.

Then say your final farewell
and return me to earth in ashes.
Whisper my name.
I will come to you.

Bay Bench

The tide creeps up the beach
and ripples softly at our feet.
We share our love
with this misty invader
as far above a stormy night sky
suddenly sets free the stars.

I smell your sweet hair.
Adore your innocent eyes.
Kiss your willing lips.
Sea-chilled, we gaze at infinity
and dare to dream.

Here was the instant
I first truly loved you – held you,
and almost cried out in fear.

In The Dunes

I slept by you that night
in a lover's bed on South Beach,
oblivious to the chill of the sand
and a sea wind joining us closer
than mere passion concedes.
Salty wetness on our shoulders,
your hair sticky symmetry,
sweet with sea dew.
Deep in the dunes
sheltered we together.

Flank Attack

It was love that brought us here
and hides us now behind the bush,
between the trees, and over the hill.
Love it was, gone wild with lust
and fevered breath on breath!
Brave we were to tempt the tiny
to a sultry taste of thigh and hiny.
Surely, none would dare…

AHHH! My God!

We trespass in passionless greenery.

Dewdrop

The earthy, roaring rush
of my gypsy sister wind
sings me
one man's measure of God,
kisses me
with heather's howl,
charms me
with autumn's crackling constant.

In a sublime delicacy
of the master's cosmos,
in a dizzy little dewdrop
lay love.
I saw it.
I saw you.

Trip South

Long, mostly brown symmetry
indulges my imagination,
falls and covers discreetly
her babe's delight.
Divine curves fashion her hips
and promise sweet surrender.

Passions abound
on an excursion
with the fowl!

When We Loved

When we loved,
the first bouquet of spring
swept up from the valley
on the breeze,
and carried a promise
of not what could be,
but must be.

When we loved,
the child souls inside
brought us to quiet waters
in the sun,
and watched the daring-do
on reservoir rocks
long patient with our play.

When we loved,
the pebble names we made
hid our hope and our being
in grassy deep,
and waited for the instant
when two would become one.

Dance With Me

Dance with me, birches,
to the Waltz of the Wind
and the fleeting sight of
pale yellow leaves
twinkling in the sun
against the blue sky.
You lead, I'll follow.
Together, we'll find God
and perhaps one day, peace.

Dreams

I am always me,
same face, same faults.
I am lost in Grand Central
trying to find my train.
My wallet is gone.
Panic.
I try to find my way home
over hills I know
and paths often walked,
but home is always too far,
the road too long.
Tired.
I see a woman. Our eyes meet.
I cannot reach her, only see her,
but I feel holiness touching me.
Joy.

I say to her, not knowing how:

You are in God's friendship
and beloved by His son.
The gifts given for your grace
are love, trust, and hope.
There are no greater gifts for the living.

Alive

You are alive.
You breathe, think,
feel, sense, intuit.

The light of God
is within you, a gift
to be opened in time.

You are alive.
The Creator is alive.
The Universe is alive.
It awaits your gift.

Let it be Love.

BEAUTY

A Man Long Gone

I stand staring at his art.
The sunrise, or is it sunset,
glows from the far horizon.
Saffron, cobalt, and cadmium
streak across the sky in waves
of blended, yet pure colors.
Ocean swells capture the rays
from the radiant orange orb.
Initials and a date remind me
that, yes, he once was here,
wondering if his art was worthy
of even a passing glance.
He is a man long gone now,
but I see how he loved beauty.

Beauty

Beauty defends God
against old logic,
new science,
all thought.

Beauty seeks beauty
in a heart,
a flower,
a shadow.

Beauty becomes beauty
when all else
is tasted,
is seen.

Search for beauty.
Create beauty.
Embrace beauty
until you cry.

Creativity

Creativity, conceived in the mind,
pursued by the heart,
expressed in a poem,
a painting, line, form, or color
is a celebration of consciousness.

Creativity, inspired by a calling
from a sense beyond self,
opposes nothingness by
arousing and renewing
the fabric of the whole.

Creativity, once imagined,
longs for expression,
contemplation, and comprehension
by kindred spirits in ages past
and yet to come.

In The Air

High against a crazy quilt sky
gone wild with rain gray clouds
streaming west over the islands,
two eagles play tag in the air.

Matching moves like airmen of old,
they dart left, feint right, then soar
to new heights, all without moving a wing.

Touching talons in an ancient salute,
they speak as only eagles can
and honor a game as old as time.

Lessons

When you realize beauty,
you honor the divine.

When you realize gratitude,
you quiet the self.

When you realize forgiveness,
you cleanse the soul.

When you realize love,
you embrace the All.

Springtime

Everything expresses the Creator
when blossoming into beauty.

Morning skies awake with blushes.
Rosy buds promise sweet perfume.
Pale greeneries hint at cool shade.
Evening sounds sing with pure joy.

Springtime is soft on the soul
and passion for the senses.

Sunrise

I crest the rise and walk into sun
that paints the shimmering bay
in scarlet red and indigo blue.

Lupine bends to the light,
sweet grass sparkles with dew,
and dainty gray birch leaves
rustle in concert as a breeze
sweeps in from the west.

A cardinal trills his greeting
and calls for a lady love
to drop down from the sky.
Hummingbirds joust and buzz
in dazzling aerial display.
An eagle circles on thermals
rising from the warming earth.

Sunrise. Beauty. Bliss.

The Days Glide By

Somewhere along the way of life,
I happened upon a moment of peace.
It was late in life one summer eve
when the sky blazed rainbow hues
and the world about hailed me
with chirps, quacks, and rustling.

It is later now, later still by years.
The days glide by like cotton ball clouds
skipping across the pale blue sky.

The Old Stone

Child, look down, look at me!
I am beautiful, I am round and very old.
For ages this rocky beach has been home.

Pick me up and admire my colors
for never will you see another so fine.

Save me from the cold, endless tides
that imprison me on this rocky shore.

Hold me, cherish me and clean me
of the salty crust I have borne so long.

Put me on a sunny windowsill
and I will charm you with memories
of white periwinkles sparkling in the foam
and cool sand swimming between your toes.

Child, I am yours now.
Let me rest forever in your heart.

The Path

God creates,
nature explains.

Spirit smiles,
mind knows.

Soul rejoices,
journey begins.

Truth In Beauty

A crisp sea breeze from the east
urges the sparkling wavelets
to break quietly on stones at my feet.
Rattling and grinding for millennia,
the granite gems gleam in the sun,
muted colors made vibrant by salty sea.

Seducing the senses with smoothing,
they long for the greatest prize –
the touch of a knowing hand,
the gaze of a loving eye,
the joy of an awakened mind
seeking truth in beauty
and God in a yearning stone.

Velvet Touch

Curves and patterns of dappled light
glide across the bay on the breeze.
The east wind gathers her skirts
and rushes headlong up the hill,
twirling the leaves of the gray birch
with a velvet touch.

Love Is One

High atop the old maple,
the wind blows cool.
Leaves glow saffron
in the last low light
and chatter a timeless farewell,
dancing their final waltz
in a shower of gold.

They whisper in passing:

Beauty is the beginning
of the end of the journey.
Seek the light within.
You will awaken it,
the beauty eternal.
Seek the light within.
The light is love.
Love is One.

Search For Beauty

Watch the firefly dance
and it will glow more brightly.

Caress the crimson tulip
and it will shiver with joy.

Rest beside the quiet brook
and it will babble blissfully.

Search everywhere for beauty
and it will kiss your soul.

Contemplations

Beauty is
the mind's perception
of perfection.

Love is
the soul's light
against the darkness.

Gratitude is
the heart's joy
in knowing
that beauty is all
and love never dies.

LOSS

Bus Stop

I remember it like yesterday
though it was back in sixty-six,
in the front seat of a fifty-four.

You came two thousand miles
to tell me that loneliness and lust
make especially fine bedfellows.
All that I was, all I pretended to be,
deserted me with your one word, *yes*.

Everything changed.
I could not find you.
I could not find me.
I was only wretched hollowness,
speechless on a muddy mountainside
somewhere north of Denver
more dead than alive.

I picked you up at midnight
and took you to the bus.
It arrived, you got on, it left.

I cannot remember if we waved goodbye.

One Song

There's only one song
that after all these years
still makes me turn
to see if you're there.

There's only one song
that pains and pleasures
when I chance to hear
the first three notes.

There's only one song
that hollows my heart
and brings hot tears
I don't want to stop.

There's only one song
that I love and fear
for the shame and sorrow
it brings to my soul.

There's only one song
that in an instant
can spin me back
to our time, our place.

There's only one song.

Autumn Without

Autumn approaches this year
with its usual fiery brilliance.
Shadow-dappled sunbeams of gold
cascade from high atop the maples
and caress the forest floor.

We came here often
to celebrate the season
and play like children
on its soft, crumbly bed.

Do you remember, too?

Love was once here and rejoiced
in the sound of our footsteps,
crackling and crunching
the colorful embrace of September.

I recall the sound instantly, too easily.
I miss the loveliness of you.

Girl Up The Hill

I taste your heart
through your tears
as you swell in
questioning and embers
giving me
your precious purity.
Lust is strong wine
when little town girls
meet big city dreams.

Where are you now?
Who are you with?
What do you love?

Perhaps we will meet again,
older, wiser and still wondering
why such sweet feelings
flowered so briefly.

I Walk By, Want To Cry

With the dawn I feel forlorn.
My sad life ebbs with strife.
Love has come, now it's done.
Easy to see you're over me.
When we kiss there's no bliss.
When we meet we don't greet.

I walk by, want to cry.

I do wonder what went asunder,
what went wrong for so long.
You won't care if I dare
seek a lover who won't discover
the tragic me you can see,
but can't cherish, lest you perish.

I walk by, want to cry.

So I'll go but you know
when I leave I'll also grieve.
In his arms, with his charms,
he'll never find my real mind,
my hidden place, my true face.
Goodbye to you who always knew.

I walk by, want to cry.

Under Oak

Come, let's borrow
each other's eyes
and exchange mists
of mutual fascination.
Lie with me
in this autumnal wonderland
and forget the coming cruelty.
The world pities not we dreamers.
Our moment seems eternally squandered,
struck senseless upon a sterile hell
of unforgiving reality.

Flannel Dawn

I have been too long
on this dampened road,
yet I shall stay somewhat longer.

In the lingering light
of a rosy dawn,
frost still clings
to the last leaves of fall.
The chickadees,
besieged by fusty wont,
ruffle their indignation
at the dearth of seeds.
The farmer's stones
in the rambling old wall
shiver under a blanket of icy moss.

I am here, you –
senseless from circumstance
and no friend to fate.

Goodbye

As I look upon her face
of singular beauty,
a cold hand
touches me softly.

Glorious azure eyes
that once embraced life
in all its goodness and light
now dim to a final obscurity
only death can manufacture.

Oh, God, are you taking her now?

A silent tear
trickles desolately
down her pale cheek.

A final, futile look
at the beckoning beyond.

She is gone.

Reflections

Amber yellow,
pale green,
chocolate brown,
burgundy red.

Like a clown
with many bright colors,
you make the people laugh.
With happy spirits,
dead spirits,
they laugh.

Away to drown
in vision rare
drift their bubbly souls.
Over cork and cap
they fly,
never to return.

Light Of A Flower

Now you live on
in the light of a flower.
In the seed
of the broom straw.
In the sweetness
of viburnum.
In the song
of a bluebird.
In the coolness
of spring.
In the fragrance
of fall.
In the breath
of summer.
In the quiet
of winter.

Take My Love With You

On the first day of summer,
the longest light of the year,
daisies shine like diamonds
in the dusk of Wednesday done.
Ferns silhouette their shadows
on nearby granite and schist
as bats turn broad circles
and hunt on silent wings.
The big dog guards me
from things I cannot see.
He pants from the humid heat
or perhaps the age of his bones.

The last of my mother
is going the way of the ages.
Soon I will be without hope
of ever feeling again
her hand on my sickly forehead,
the comfort of her encouraging words,
the promise of a favorite meal
made only as a mother can.

Take my love with you
on your journey to the light.

This Dog Beside Me

This dog beside me
walks more slowly now.
He does not hear so well.
He sleeps away the day
dreaming of chases past.
He is my best friend,
confidant, and protector.
He owes me nothing.
I have never loved so purely.
I fear the coming grief.

Someday

Someday,
touched by a breath from the past,
a familiar sound on the wind,
a walk to your favorite spots,
I will turn to look for you,
but you will not be there.

I will not have your watchful eyes,
the whirling joy at my return,
the big pink tongue tickling my ear,
the loyalty, the devotion, the being.

But I will have the memories,
and I will have the love.
And that must be enough.

Snow-White Sneakers

The old man creeps carefully
down the driveway hill.
His back is bent with years,
and his feet bound tightly
with snow-white sneakers.
Baggy trousers with no belt
and a clean tan shirt
dangle from his thinning frame.
He opens the mailbox door
hoping to find a sign
that someone, anyone,
remembers him.
He stares at the vacancy
with sadness and disbelief.
He looks away and wonders
if he already picked up the mail.

Our eyes meet as I stride by.
He turns and ambles up his hill.
I can tell. He is alone.

GRATITUDE

Hold Onto The Days

The years of my life are passing.
I know that now for certain,
in ways the young can never fathom,
until they, too, open time's curtain
and sense the final act has begun.
I hold onto the days dearly
when I knew my mother's love
and heard my father's laugh.
I walk the old dirt roads
so full of memories of dogs, girls, the barn,
maple trees, birds at the feeder, fields,
school buses, cap guns, sitters,
the sand bank, the cemetery,
and the grandfather I knew so briefly.

Late in my years, I seem trapped
in the past, maudlin with memories
of what I was before my life.
It was simpler, lighter,
without the weight of shame.
I miss it terribly, or could it be
that I simply miss the love?

(continued on the next page)

There is no going back, no starting over.
Choices--not chance—make a life,
perhaps with a nudge from Fate.
It takes a lifetime to know this.
In the years that I have still,
I will walk often in old footsteps
from another time, a younger soul.
I will seek forgiveness
for cruelties that came too easily
from the darkest parts of me.
I will listen to what the light is saying.
I will be thankful for every single day.

Days Given

The days turn more quickly now
as the season moves anew.
The sun creeps south from east.
The north wind sets afire
golden leaves of quaking aspen.
Honkers bid farewell from on high.
Monarchs cling briefly to fading petals.
Susans sway in yellow bouquets.
Crickets announce the coming chill.
Reds and grays scurry to fill larders.

I witness this precious gift of time
ever grateful for days given.

"Hee Did It"

The spring song of the chickadee
sings in sweet harmony with
the rain softly pelting my roof.
The tiny bird adds three notes
to the concert and reminds me
how grateful I am for a life of
hearing
seeing
feeling
being
loving.
Nature speaks in eloquent simplicity.
Embrace her. Listen.

Blessed

It's the things in the background of our living
that determine who were are, and what we cherish.

I hear bumble bees in the barberry bushes,
a wren chattering from somewhere afar,
and the cardinal who wakes me up every morning
is still pining for a lady friend to love.

The spring-green grass invites me to rest on its soft bed.
We have been friends since infancy.

The high tide in the bay yields a quiet silver blue.
There is no wind to disturb its reflections of sky and tree.

The quaking aspen twinkles with early leaves
and reminds me of days gone by in a distant state of mind.

The dwarf irises delight in rows of deep purple,
and poppies and peonies promise brilliant delights.

These things are my rock, my memories, my now.
I count myself blessed.

Precious

Today I see.
Fragile is the breath between living and dying.
Joyous is the red wing caroling a spring surprise.
Gentle is the raindrop dripping on a fern.

Lovely are the memories of then and when.
Everything is more precious than yesterday.

Living Is The Gift

First, birth.
Then, life.
Last, death.

Rejoice, then, in
the in-between:
the searching,
the finding,
the certainty
that living is the gift –
and gratitude, salvation.

The heart will ever rest
when the thirst for beauty
is nobly quenched,
love trusted as passion
and compassion,
forgiveness finally given.

Be grateful for the senses.
Savor all the flavors.
Confront the many demons.
Go quietly with no regrets.

You Thank Us With Flowers

Come spring, new lupine appears
at her head, her breast, her feet
where last year we saw only moss,
grass, and a hint of meadow blossoms.

We honor you, Millie Johnson White,
as we raise your gravestone
and place it where your children did
so many years ago, atop the knoll
that looks over the bay you loved.

We walk your land, sow your field,
feel your breezes, warm in your sun.
You thank us with flowers soon to be
aglow in muted, beautiful colors
of the earth, sky, and sunrises to come.

They will remind us that to everything,
there is a season.

FORGIVENESS

Listening To Dusk

Purple twilight quiets a horizon
still aflame with the spirits of day.
Leaves spill from high reaches
and clatter like rain, only deeper.
Bittersweet breezes seed the dusk
with the ancient fragrance of time.

We are born of light and darkness.
From love, faith, and knowledge
conscience must prevail.

Lessons learned late in life
promise the gift of forgiveness.

Free Of Me

All this time I have wanted,
searched, floundered, succeeded.
Now all I want is to be free of me,
of sin, guilt, regret, and what ifs.

I want sadness to be a memory
confined to the back of my mind.

I want love to carry me heavenward
on wings that will never fail me.

Most of all, I want forgiveness.
But the burden is heavy, the road long,
and the toll at the Gates unknown.

Confession

Velvet green grass
welcomes the dawn
with dazzling diamonds
of sun-soaked dew.

The morning breeze
is heavy with the spice
of summer creation.

I come here grateful
for the comfort of
fireplace flames
dancing to Mozart violins,
nocturnes of Chopin
defining the sublime,
and quaint field flowers
snuggling in the fog
to confess my sins
and ask for forgiveness.

Take Me

The bees dance to the blossoms.
The leaves of the chestnut signal a breeze.
The light blends silver beyond.

There is not much left of me.
I see the depth of it now.
I ask again for forgiveness.

I am tired.
You may take me.
I need your love.
I need forgiveness.
I need redemption.

Do the leaves now celebrate?
Does the light seem more beautiful?
Why am I breathing so lightly?

Beauty found me on a path to the sea.
Had I been unworthy in the quest,
it surely would have passed me by.
I can feel its embrace.
The burden is now lighter.

I am smiling. I am smiling!
I have been given redemption.
I have been forgiven by beauty.

DISCOVERY

The Telling

Seek beauty in this life
for in seeing glory,
you glimpse the everything.

Honor those who came before
for in cherishing ages past,
you remember yourself.

Love the music of your heart
for in hearing the songs,
you know the words.

Believe in the sublime
for in surrendering to trust,
you are free to dream.

Find perfect silence
for in hearing nothing,
you begin the journey.

Silence

Stillness, quiet absolute,
is a gift only given
when you find it.

You will hear
no breath of wind,
no song of bird,
no cry of child,
no laugh of lover,
no sound at all
but your heart
beating in rhythm
with the whole.

You can rest in silence.
You can see in silence.

Song Of The Leaf

You need only look to the leaf
to grasp the why of the world.
You are conceived in pleasure,
a bud where once was none.
You spring to life in light,
blessed by warmth and sun.
You blossom to beauty and love
in the sweet song of summer.
You share your splendor with all
in the quiet of autumn days.
You fall to earth and rest
in the cool embrace of winter.
You nurture the well of life
until you return again.

Connections

With each new year that passes
I see the Way more clearly.

Dancing yellow daffodils.
Slippery crimson tulips.
Green grass sodden
with sudden rain.
Lichen laughing
at the touch of the sun.
Spring buds bending
to the western breeze.
Birds welcoming the light
with song.

They call to me.
See, they ask.
Feel, they wish.
Touch, they offer.
Listen, they want.
Do these things
and you will know
the way of the world.

We are all One.

Sudden Wind

I heard it first in the pines.
I heard the wind before I saw it.
I saw the wind before I felt it.
I watched it come at me
like some wild unchecked thing
bending branches,
scattering snow and leaf dust,
and howling its power
at a solitary figure, me.

It came out of nowhere.
I waited for its touch.
It brushed by in a hurry
and carried a message
only I could hear.

We Are Everything

The Dipper's coming round again,
and with it the promise of spring.
It rises triumphant over the black sky,
each night ever higher in hope.

Three handle stars trim the branches
of the soaring elm and spidery maple.
Four ladle stars capture new buds
in the cradle of Charlemagne's Wain.

Another year of sensing passes,
far quicker than the last.
Another year of seeing
more than ever before.
Another year of longing
for time and stillness.
Another year of learning
we are everything.

Ancient Eyes Imagining

With ancient eyes imagining,
I gaze across the valley of forever.
Time blushes pink with envy
as I rest again on this gray granite,
warmed by the touch of sunlight.

Through distant ages long forgotten
I have always found my way here,
as a child, as a lover, as a warrior.
It has changed little over the millennia.
It remains a beacon on the mountain
that cries a joyous song of greeting
at the touch of my familiar hand.

I stay the day and at dusk I pray:
You are my place of being,
my way to the knowing,
my promise of the joining.
You are the rock upon which
I will search for the whole.

As Is A Flower

As is a flower,
birthing,
budding,
blossoming,
seeding,
quieting,
passing,
birthing,
as is Man
until He sees.

After The Grace

The light of a sepia dawn
paints the leaves in rusty olive
and wakens me to questions
of what and how and why.

What do I do with the grace?

Hiding beneath the branches
of the great maple tree
gone all glorious with sun,
I feel nature's embrace.
I see that everything is divine.

What do I do with the grace?

I will search for beauty
in ways I longed to as a child.
I will capture the instant
when light and shadow and color
waltz to the music of time.
I will write of the light within.

Realization

Stand beneath a spray of maple
hued green with golden spring,
as high aloft a cathedral sways
in the warm morning breeze.

Each season anew
this simple parson
strives ever higher,
spreads ever wider
to touch the light of life,
to join the essence of one.

I am humbled by the sermon.

Sit beneath a dappled sky
as amber and azure and pearl
parade to stillness and dusk
in the cool evening breeze.

It is there. I am here.
It is fathomless. I am tiny.
It is beautiful. I am human.
It is good. I am unworthy.
It is forgiving. I am comforted.
It is alluring. I am tempted.
It is everything. I am part.

I am humbled by the sermon.

Journey

I saw a single star
take two paths
on my journey down the river.

I felt my old soul
greet my heart
as I walked the ancient trail.

I heard a silent grace
sing to me
on a night black with wonder.

I watched a life path
complete its journey
at the falls of the gorge.

I glimpsed the whole
offer an instant
to comprehend the why.

I see our connection.
I feel across the ages.
I hear beyond the quiet.
I watch destiny find belonging.
I glimpse the oneness.

If I have found God,
if by seeing I am seen,
if this is my end on Earth,
let me linger in this beauty
a moment longer.

Mirror

At
the
end
of
a
true
journey
of
faith
is
a
mirror
reflecting
the
face
of
God.

I Am Free

Spring green swims
in Heaven's gray twilight.
The night bird sings
a love song to the dusk.
The cool breeze bids me
to stay and listen.

It is the instant I know I am free.

The wind may carry me afar,
but I am unafraid
for I am everything.

I am here, and I am not.
I am free to leave,
free to breathe the breath of forever.

A Prayer's Journey

The universe
is like the water
of an eternal sea.
Even a single prayer
sends a ripple
across the breadth
of the whole,
and on its journey
rings a bell
of sublime purity
for God to hear.

God is everything.
God *is*.
Seek God.
You will find the way.

Essence

Called by the turning of seasons
and brilliant in final display,
the leaf pirouettes quietly to earth,
cradled in the arms of the wind.

I breathe the same air
that has touched the leaf,
brushed the wet bark,
swept over the stonewall
and bent the grass.

All that they are, I am.

The essence of man –
the passion of the heart,
the colors of the mind,
the tears of the soul,
the light and dark within –
rejoice at the seeing.

Becoming

To discover your self,
lose your self
and search in places where
intuition leads to yearning.

To see behind the veil,
go blind to a dance
where the rhythm of creation
hides in plain sight.

Look up! Look up!
The night sky beckons!
Can you see? Can you see?
You are everything
that has ever been
and will ever be.

Just Beyond

There is a purity,
a lightness of light,
a lifting of the veil,
that is just beyond.
It awaits you to
find it in the quiet,
feel it in your heart,
know it in your mind.

Rhythms

Where the sunlight
breaks through the branches
and brightens the leaves,
a thousand tiny flyers swirl
like a school of fish in the sea.
Seeking the comfort of the light,
they are blown by the breeze
and scatter like sand in a storm.
Twirling and diving in unison,
the great writhing flock
rises in rhythm back to the light.
Some brave souls steal away,
tiny specks in the void of air.
Round and round they fly,
tasting life outside the whole.
One by one, they return
to the dancing swarm,
sparkling now in the grace
of a dusky September sun.

Could life be this simple?
We come from the light we love.
In living, we stray from our mother.
In death, we return to her love.

Invitation From A Stone

Sunlight hides behind the maple.
It is quiet but for a breeze.
The great gray stone calls to me,
not once, but twice.
It straddles the quiet waters
of a small stream
bubbling down the hillside.

I sit in peace and wonder.

God is. I am.
I am what I am.
Am I unworthy?

God is perfect.
Flesh is imperfect,
clouding the light within.

Only when
doubt
is a distant memory,
shame
a discarded garment,
desire
a glowing ember,
forgiveness
a familiar path,
will yearning become being.

Light Under Leaves

Sunset.
The great orb plummets
behind ebony tree trunks
garden-thick in the grove beyond.
The last leaves of oak and maple
kindle in gold, lit from below
by light under leaves.

Dusk descends as
the last of the day meets
the first of the night.

When you find yourself,
and the answer you seek,
it will come from knowing
that you are the leaves,
and the light, and the dark.

Inside Dusk

Let your mind go.
Listen.
Look up to the maple boughs.
You see dimension, depth.
Look longer. Deeper.
You see only a single plane.
Everything is bound
by everything else.
Light and dark exist equally
in the fabric of existence.

Ever To Create

The soul is the lifeblood of all existence.
It rests within the fevered heart of man
until called by a timeless yearning,
a divine migration to rejoin the whole
and create, ever to create.

Thoughts Upon Cavalry

Someone feel with me
the presence of Jesus tonight!

Come, climb to the top
of this hideous eminence
and know that at its summit,
we, unlike Him,
will live to see the sun again.

In His name millions perished.
In His name millions found peace.

Who among you can say in truth
that His legacy is not in opposites?

It takes faith to believe in Him.
It takes knowledge to see beyond Him.

You do not need Jesus to see God.

Halloween Alone

Sad I was, and alone as well,
as October's yawing gusts
lanced the last leaves from summer stem.
Orange orb, it's time to face
your bastard annual call.

Will they come? Will they come?

I gave you eyes and big teeth, too,
and a smile that would not scare.
Then wait we did like father and son
to see who took our dare.

Will they come? Will they come?

Crusading slivers of my aureate candle Christ
flickered, beckoned, begged through the night
for tiny sharers of the seasonal superstition.

Will they come? Will they come?

A gentle gypsy knock laced with cackle
butchered the gloom, burst through the room!
I stayed by Him, comforted Him,
till His waxen beacon burned to the Fall.

Hollowtown

Naked November treetops
bend to the bidding
of an icy west wind,
come down from Canada
to freeze the faces
of wealthy walkers
strolling on the street
of a tiny little town
where you'd love to live,
but can't make the cut
in the cliquey country club,
and where people in the pews
of the charming little church
worship each Sunday and wonder
why there's no peace in prayer.

Police Report

Johnny Walker,
big talker.
Drinking beer,
didn't hear
Jackie Black
in back
of store.
"She's a whore!"
Johnny said.
Turned red
when Stan,
Jackie's man,
stepped out
to shout,
"Better run!
My gun
gonna pain
your brain!"
Next day
far away
Walker found,
face down
bloody head,
very dead.

The Ancient One

You are four sides smooth
from grinding sweet dried corn.

A thousand years ago and more
you slipped from the woman's hand.
You tumbled from high cliff village
spinning and bounding with joy.

You clattered down the sandstone
and rolled to a nook in the shale,
free once again and with friends.
There beneath the fragrant sage
you lay hidden from the woman
and the children sent to find you.

The air you breathed,
the rain you drank,
the cold you bore,
the sun you welcomed
as you waited the turn of centuries.
No hand would touch you until mine.
Surely you were her favorite
for you are small and round and sturdy.

Woman, I hold your stone in my hand!
I remember you and greet you through time.

Sad With The World

I search for beauty and find it
in remote, ever smaller preserves.

I hear it in the spring warble
of red-winged blackbirds.

I smell it in the sweet perfume
of sunny tulips standing tall.

I touch it in the dimpled bark
of budding beech and maple.

I feel it in the moist rush
of April winds at sundown.

I see it in the yellow splendor
of swaying daffodils open wide.

I do not see it in the eyes of men
murdering children in God's name.

The Dove

One minute you are flying free,
cooing a love song and savoring my seed.
An instant later you are crippled,
crumpled on the ground, a mass of gray down.
An April snow has found you hungry
but a hungry hawk has found you!
In needle-sharp talons you are plucked from the sky,
but blue jays protest and crows pursue
and the hunter drops you limp to my land.
You bleed red in the snow, sniffed by dogs
who know when death rides in on the wind.
You blink at me through dazed eyes
and flutter a weak escape.
There is so little time, I know.
I take you to your final rest.
I turn your back to the sky
so you may rest your head
and spread your wings.
I stay with you
to protect the dignity of your dying.
You struggle against the blackness
or perhaps you strive for the light.
You blink at me and tuck your head
beneath your bloodied breast.
You arch your feathers in a final farewell
and with a great shudder befitting an eagle,
you leave this earth and join the whole.
Perhaps I was some comfort at the end.
Perhaps you knew I was praying.
Dear God, take the soul of this sweet dove
into your heart. Thank you. Amen.

Just A Moment Ago

Just a moment ago,
July breezes carried you
over wildflowers sticky-sweet
with summer's bounty.
Now you lie in the road,
dead from the strike of a car.

Your mate walks to your side.
Tiny feet touch yours, hoping you
will rise and fly beside him again.
In a ritual older than time,
he shields you with swallowtail wings
and says goodbye the only way he knows.

I take you from the road.
I put you in tall grass
so your beauty will join the earth.

I watch your mate continue his journey
to somewhere and forever.
It is how it must be.

I realize that even in the smallest creatures,
love exists.

Mocs

Put a pair of moccasins
on your bare feet.
Walk on the grass, in the woods,
wherever your heart sends you.
Feel beneath your toes and heels
the bumps, the points, the lines
of roots, clods, leaves, and stones.

As you rest beneath the dipper
and love by the light of the moon,
consider this: Nature is not perfect.
It is not polished smooth
by the hand of man.
No convenience is intended here,
no sanded floor, concrete road,
or parquet marble entrance.
Nature is free to move with time,
to change with the seasons
as she sees fit.

It began this way.
It will end this way.

Sunset

Life: A brilliant sunset.
It lasts a breath, sometimes two.

Pink hues of young love
turn to streaks of quiet gray.

Passion, so pure, so fleeting,
flickers, then dims.

Memories linger, some joyful,
others black with shame.

It is enough to know love,
find beauty, fight darkness.

Only when you are old
do memories of your days
yield such wisdom.

The Road

However one may seek grace,
let him walk that road.

The destination,
not the journey
nor the means
nor the prophet
should transcend
the realization.

Intolerance is intolerable
in matters of faith.

NIGHTS

Cloudy Blue Adagio

The land is a quiet of cloudy blue
hushed by the kiss of moonlight.
Lovelorn cicadas pine in adagio,
chilled by the turning of earth.
The little brook giggles a soft hello,
then wanders away with a trickle.
No wind dares to rattle the leaves;
it is a perfect night for listening.

It is a perfect night for seeing
beyond the boundaries of me.
I see line, not form.
I see contrast, not conformity.
I see whirls and whorls, not points.
I see infinite imaginings of pale lace
in silent silhouette with the night sky.

I walk in wonder in a world of shadows.

Coyote Cantata

To know yourself, walk in quiet
on a night when Queen Anne's lace
captures the starlight in its willowy arms
and shines it back to the heavens.

Go, discover a place that calls to you
on the grass,
by the brook,
in the woods,
on an old stonewall.

Sit in silence as long as you dare
and ask for the wisdom that comes
from opening your mind to eternity.

Listen to the sound of the land breathing,
the ballad of the bug,
the cantata of the coyote,
the ode of the owl,
the whistle of the west wind
sifting the boughs of evergreens.

Look for comfort to the night sky
and know you are never alone.

Moon Trees

The moon comes up
behind bare branches,
swaying to the cool caress
of the evening wind.
Touching first a trunk,
then a crooked bend
last a feathered summit,
it rises in ecstasy
on a steel blue horizon,
a gold diamond in the night
shimmering in light so bright
the stars quiet in envy.
I am alone
watching this timeless waltz,
aware that in the silence
I can hear my soul sing.

Gift Of The Night

It is the
randomness
of the
raindrops
on my tent
that so enchants me.

There is no
rhythm.
And yet there is
song
of nature's divine chaos.

Charlemagne's Wain

From ancient times beyond imagining
when only rocks were here,
the heavens showcased every night
your beauty far and near.

Of all the shapes of gold and glitter
that in the night sky shine,
one it is that man knows best,
the one I claim as mine.

For in my soul I carry deep
the prayers, the praise, the dreams
of every eye that ever gazed
upon your sparkling beams.

I speak for Man, and gladly so
because I love the past.
Shine you bright, Big Dipper,
until we breathe our last.

Perspectives

You know lilac in spring,
glorious in lavender
and bursting with a bouquet
that heralds the scented season.

You see lilac in three dimensions
but it is loveliest in one.

To see the hand of creation
drawing the art of light,
look at lilac's shadow
pressed against the clapboard
by the neon light of a full moon.

Epitaph

The old man and the dog
don't walk by anymore.
He told us to remember him
on a night like this,
when hurricane clouds
chase each other across the sky,
dancing like celestial children
to the music of a blue moon.
Listen always to your heart
and the song it needs to sing, he said.
Who's that whispering?
It's nobody, just the wind.
Breathe deeply of fallen leaves
warmed by October sun, he said.
Who's that talking?
It's nobody, only the rain.
Treasure the silence of snowy woods
broken only by your footsteps, he said.
Who's that speaking?
It's nobody, nobody at all.
Rejoice when your eyes first see
the pale green coming of spring, he said.
What was that sound?
It's nothing, just my heart beating.
Feel the sun upon your face
as summer serenades in color, he said.
Who are you?
I am everything you love.

Gauze On The Moon

Spring came in with a snowstorm,
blowing wet and heavy with sleet.
The squall, so sudden and swift,
bent low the spruce bough and pine,
and buried our snowdrops and crocus
under a varnish of crystal white.

Who could have known last night
when we walked the parched path
that a wish to the moon would come true?

Lifting a glass to the change of seasons
we greeted the crescent in the west
through a gauze of gray and mist.
It smiled back like a Cheshire cat
stalking the ripe buds of maples.

Who could have known last night
that we said a prayer for water?

SEASONS

The Turning

It happens every year,
in one brief instant,
when the few animal senses that remain
sing loudly of the turning.

A breath upon your face,
light and wet.

Rosy tips of ripening buds
begging to let loose their color.

The earthy musk of land
feasting on last season's leaves.

Chattering red wings aloft in the elm
and chickadees calling for love.

Your face turned up to the sun.

And if you know the turning well,
a stillness in the air that lasts a heartbeat,
yet in the instant of its being
trumpets that spring is here.

Broom Straw In Snow

You are unspoiled,
awaiting a lover
to savor your charms.
You are symmetry,
swaying softly
to the kiss of the wind.
You are color,
butterscotch
blended by the earth and sun.
You are shape,
divine curves
drawn by the eons.
You are texture,
delicate stems
to feathered tops.
You are contrast,
shadows of gold
on pristine white.
You are smell,
fragrant with spice
of sleeping earth.
You are sound,
ruffled by hint
of sudden breeze.
You are light,
waltzing in harmony
with sparkles.
You are music,
whispering a symphony
to only a few.

So Far To Travel

Monarch in twilight,
first one and now two!
Ghost lovers gliding
through September chill,
you are silent shadows
weaving the wind
over branch and under leaf
looking to land.

Stop here, please
on your journey to the jungle.
Sleep among my trees
and within my dreams.

Rest for a night
and come morning's gray light,
drink from the dew
of my sweet pink phlox
and be gone.

Stop now.
Rest here.
You have so far to travel.

Honkers

They bring the season with them,
in flocks gliding down from on high,
tooting their coming with excited hellos,
wings whistling a beat through the sky.

Over my head with a great whoosh-whoosh
they make for the lake down the hill,
to cackle and babble as good friends do
till dusk, when they know to be still.

On a winter eve 'tis magic to hear
the faint calls of honkers in flight,
as high above they touch the stars
and wing swiftly through dark of night.

I've also seen a sight so rare
that few men believe the telling,
of wings lifted up by the gold of the sun
setting low cross the land in evening.

Great goose above, you touch my soul
and your song reaches parts of me
that are ancient, pure, and yearning
for before, and what's still to be.

The Flight Of Seasons

Through my windowpane I see
four seasons come and go.
I watch each tiny bud and leaf
sprout high where once was low.

A year is birthing and through the pale
comes life where once seemed dead.
April colors I love the best,
when black twigs turn to red.

Summer paints the world all green,
then fall changes everything.
The dark of winter stays not long
but lifts each day toward spring.

A gift it is to see the splendors
that pass with the flight of seasons,
to feel akin to Mother Earth
and share with you my reasons.

In Between Time

It is when everything starts to sleep,
resting from summer's long show.
Nothing seems truly alive
but stray blades of green grass,
and lingering leaves
and bittersweet berries
ripening and peeling in the sun.

It is when naked branches
rattle and clatter in the north wind
and frost paints the stems and buds
from a palette of crystal and ice.

It is when the belt of Orion
still rides low on the horizon
and islands of cloudy cotton
scamper across the stars,
lifted high by moonlight
and so close to Heaven.

Tumble Down

November early, just after dawn.
I hear the great goose saluting the stars
from a height I cannot imagine.
First frost came last night,
hitching a ride on the north wind.
Morning sun rouses the crimson
and stirs the saffron from frozen sleep.
Beauty yields to time.
Leaves tumble down.
One after the other,
now in pairs,
finally a waterfall
of fairy mist and hue!
Rattling, bouncing,
spinning, floating,
they sing their last song,
remembered by me,
embraced by the divine.

Autumn Concert

August is in full concert tonight!
Dog day harvest flies sizzle
through a canopy of leaves
damp from the afternoon rain.
In splendid accompaniment,
katydids beat the humid air
with a stereo vibrato largo
that pulses through the dark
like nature's fevered breathing.
The last lightning bugs streak by
hoping to discover
an eager lady in waiting
before the seasonal sleep.

I share this with you and the dogs
who sit quietly sniffing the wind,
surrounded by beauty and love.

Morning Spring

I am reminded again this year
how much I treasure
the sounds of morning spring.

Warbling from the treetops.
Tweeting from the bushes.
Twitting from the feeder.
Cries from the skies.

All these delicacies mix purely
with the scent of sublime viburnum
hanging heavy in the morning dew,
perfuming the breeze.

CHILD

Only So Many Seasons

I walk among the fireflies
or perhaps they are summer stars,
come down to play a game of tag
by the sliver of a silver moon.
In the light that yields to shadow
as the Earth starts to sleep anew,
sweet breezes ferry the musk of night
and tickle the maples to whispering.
Phantoms streak from the old elm tree
and waltz on the gauze of gray.
Sizzle bugs sing and bats ply the skies
as the woods bid farewell to the day.

Spring skies paint a robin-egg blue
and apple trees bright as white.
Lilacs birth purple, tulips burn scarlet
and daffodils blush full with sun.
Buttercups bloom from spindly sprouts
where soon grass will be velvet-green.
Peepers serenade with a rapture of song
as dusk turns to umber and teal.

Listen, child, to the colors of your years.
There are only so many seasons.

Stonewall

This old stonewall has much to tell
if you'll find a cool seat
on its lichen-covered stones.
They make a promise if you do:
The air will quiet,
the sky will blue,
the sun will warm,
and the rocks will tell their tales
of times that came before.
Look out over this land, they say.
Listen until you hear.
Imagine until you see.
Once, this field of straw was a forest
of hickory and maple and oak.
Dogwoods delicate with rosy blossoms
dotted the darkness beneath the canopy.
White birch flashed among the shadows
and burned gold in the late autumn light.
Lowing herds of black spotted cows
mingled with white tailed deer,
gorging their fill as they roamed the hill.
Blue jays warned, field mice scurried,
chickadees hid and mourning doves cooed
as red tails hunted on thermals high.
Long thin lines of sweet summer corn
marched up and down each knoll and gully,
in perfect rows like soldiers on parade.

Look carefully now, child.
Soon, we'll have only the memories.

Perhaps

And so, child, you've come to talk
to the old man grown all gray,
to hear what he might presume to know
about life, and love, and God.

Think of a diamond perfect and bright,
far older than time itself.
In ages past and all to come,
each time it sparkles anew
a life goes forth on a journey
to know itself,
to grow itself,
to return and find the whole.

It passes through birth and knows life.
It feels love, shame, pain, and joy.
It learns something it must
and perhaps a little more.

In the end it wants only
to give of itself
and in the giving,
become the whole.

Those Who Came Before

Come now, child, take my hand
and go listen with me to the night.
Walk in silence through streaks of blue
and wave to your gossamer gray shadow.
Sit with me on this ancient stone
still warm from the setting sun.
Lay your hands on its rounded top
and greet those who came before.
Listen to leaves falling one-by-one
as frost flies in on the wind,
and acorns loosening and tumbling
from twig to branch to earth.
Smell the spice of centuries past
buried round this great old stone.

Sit quietly, child, for a moment more
and open your mind to the ages.

Painted In Pearl

The world is beautiful in white
as swirls of snowflakes
wobble and tumble to earth
in a silent concerto of grace.

Painted in pearl, tree branches
prance and parade new curves,
daring to display their charms:
A soaring salute from the elm,
a cute curtsey from the birch,
a bending bow from the maple.

Child, look up with wonder!
Such perfect shapes and lines
are not drawn by mortal hands
but by snow and wind and chance.

Sing A Song Of Shadows

See a stonewall in the light of day
and you will admire its beauty.
See a stonewall painted by moonbeams
and you will hear it singing.

Wait for a night when the light is bright
and the land is all charcoal and blue.
Watch the stones glide down in granite
through shadows of mulberry and maple.
Then gently, child, go touch the stones
and ask for their chorus to rise,
and if your hand and heart are true,
you will know stones in moonlight.

They will sing a song of shadows
of old hands bent and broken
that dug them from the dark and dust
and gave the gift of sun.

They will sing a song of shadows
for those who know to listen.

Mystery In The Wind

Science may believe
there's little left to know,
but I will tell you now, child,
there's mystery in the wind.

You need only listen…
as the howl of winter
quiets to whispers of spring.

You need only hear…
as summer thunderstorms
lash demons from the dark.

You need only feel…
the frosty embrace of fall
rustling the palette of leaves.

Child, close your eyes.
Touch the wind.
Remember.

A Good Life

To you, inquiring child,
now grown old enough
to ask the why of it,
I answer what I know.

A good life,
a life truly worth living,
would be to search for
and discover for yourself
these beautiful things:

Light, truth, and love.

WRITINGS

A Boy's Prayer

The boy snuggled under the covers until the chill left him. As he began his prayers, he wondered, as he often did, if God would hear them.

He finished his prayers and decided to ask God a question he had been thinking about for a long time. "God, why am I here?"

The boy waited and waited but God did not answer him. Soon he fell asleep and started to dream.

In his dream, the boy imagined that he was sitting atop a large boulder overlooking a vast mountain range in the distance. Below him stretched a beautiful valley that appeared to have no end. The boulder he was sitting on was warm from the rays of the sun. He sat very still and listened as the wind came up from the valley and rustled the leaves in nearby trees.

A moment later he heard a voice. He looked around but saw no one. Then he heard the voice more clearly saying, "You are a gift. You will give a gift in return."

The boy was frightened when he heard the voice but found the courage of youth to ask, "I do not understand. What do you mean when you say I am a gift?"

"I gave you the gift of life," the voice answered. "You are an immortal soul within a mortal body. Your soul is a part of me."

"Are you God?" the boy asked.

"I am the Creator. All things come from me and all things must return to me."

"What gift will I give you in return?"

"You will be free to choose the path of your life until it ends. You will experience joy, sorrow, love, fear, yearning, surrender, completeness. You will know beauty and feel the darkness press hard against the light. All these emotions you will give to your soul which is a part of me."

"What happens when I die?"

"Your body will become dust and nurture the earth, but your soul will return to me with your life experiences. That is the gift you will give in return for living. Your experiences will nourish me and inspire me to create, for creation is the lifeblood of the world. As long as your soul needs to, it may return to the living until the time it wants nothing more but to join the Whole for time everlasting."

"Then will I become a star like my Granny said?" the boy asked.

"Yes, and more. You will be a part of everything that has ever been, and will ever be."

Days later, when he visited his Granny, the boy told her the dream story. She listened carefully and then rose slowly to retrieve something from a bookcase. The boy saw that it was a very old photo album with pictures in black and white. Turning the pages, Granny stopped and held the album so the boy could see a photograph. It showed a young girl in a pretty dress sitting on a large boulder. Beyond the great stone was a huge valley filled with trees.

"Granny, that's the same stone I was sitting on in my dream!" the boy exclaimed.

"Yes, child, I know, and the little girl in this picture was me."

"Granny, what does it mean? Why did I dream of you when you were young and sitting on the same stone?"

" It is a gift of love, child, from God to you. You must be an old soul who has visited this beautiful place in a past life," Granny answered, "and I have always loved it, too. It is where I used to seek God's help and blessing when I was troubled. I have not been back there for years now."

"Granny, where is this beautiful place?" the boy asked.

She turned her head to the boy and smiled brightly. "Why, it's only a short walk down our old dirt road. With your hand to help me, I think I can still make it there. Will you come with me?"

"Yes, yes, whenever you're ready, Granny! I can't wait to see it."

"You know, if you feel like it, you can offer a prayer when you are sitting on the stone."

The boy thought for a moment and said, "I'll try to think of one as we walk, okay?"

When they reached the place, the boy scrambled up to the top of the boulder while Granny watched. He looked across the valley and up to the sky and said a prayer out loud. "Dear God, Creator of all things and maker of Heaven and Earth, thank you for this day."

"Oh child, I think He would like that prayer very much!" Granny said.

A Reason For Being

In the beginning, the realm of the Creator (It) was beautiful in its vastness, glorious in its promise. But the Creator came to realize that Its realm, and therefore Itself, was incomplete and therefore imperfect. It was empty of the spiritual guideposts and experiences the Creator longed for and needed to fulfill Its own destiny.

Though all-powerful, the Creator could find nothing that was able to fill this void and bring perfection to Its realm. Since It could not manufacture spiritual ascendancy on Its own -- for such existential experiences do not exist until they are lived -- the Creator reasoned that by seeding the heavens with sentient beings who in many ways mirrored Itself, and providing them with a path for spiritual fulfill-ment, Its realm would become perfected.

To these beings It gave three precious gifts: a soul, conscious-ness, and free will. The soul was a spark of the Creator, a light within the body guarded by the heart and waiting to be discovered. Consciousness was the awareness of the promise of the quest. Free will enabled any desired path to be chosen. Thus, the Creator gave the tools humanity needed in order to become more like It.

In making the journey to understanding, we prosper spiritually in our lifetime, and upon physical death, return our soul to the Creator with the experiences of our life. If our soul has not attained realiza-tion in one life, it can reincarnate until it becomes fully perfected.

The Creator gives each of us this opportunity of knowing our reason for being. By serving the Creator, we serve ourselves and remain with the Creator as It achieves Its true destiny -- Wholeness and absorption into Eternity.

The Imperative Of Heaven

Before her passing, many of you prayed to ask for a miracle. With profound faith and humility, you asked that she be spared, healed, and restored to the beautiful, laughing, caring woman you knew and loved. You believed this could happen.

Now that she is free from the pain of this earthly life, do you *still* believe? Do you trust that God, Jesus, or the Fates do hear prayers and do create miracles?

If your answer is "yes," you are blessed with the greatest of gifts... an abiding faith that will not be broken despite the fact that your prayers were apparently unanswered. Perhaps you believe that God needed her now and had something special for her to do. Such a thought is very comforting to many who grieve over the passing of a loved one.

However, if your answer is "no" or "maybe," I ask you to consider this:

Every prayer is heard...and every prayer is answered, but not always in the here and now.

If your prayer fits the Imperative of Heaven -- the inexorable Way of time, intent, and fate -- you will witness the result.

If your prayer does not fit the Imperative of Heaven and is not obviously granted, it is *still* answered because, like every prayer, it is delivered directly to the soul of the person you are praying for. There it is treasured and adds powerful tools of strength, joy, health, and love to the everlasting soul.

So do not despair if your prayer does not seem to have the desired effect. Know for certain that the person you are praying for will carry and prosper from your prayer for time eternal.

The End.